THE *POSITIVELY QUIT!*™ MANUAL

Published by Positively Quit 2011

ISBN: 978-981-08-7417-9

For more information send an email to cas@positivelyquit.org.

Sweet words for the Positively Quit Manual

"Cheong addresses everything I know from my experience that works and doesn't work. As a psychologist, I'm impressed with how relevant research, addiction principles, and psychological tools are all covered in easy-to-read, everyday language."

Mary R. Bast, Ph.D., Personal Coach & Mentor

"Cassius Cheong has done a marvelous job of (1) identifying essential cognitive, behavioral, social/situational, and biological elements of the smoking habit, (2) distilling these down to very manageable proportions, then (3) turning it into a smoking cessation plan."

Dr. Carl G. Hindy, Clinical Psych., Nashua, NH

"This manual simply but systematically lays out a cognitive framework of the psychology of smoking, and then a multi-pronged approach to identifying why a person smokes and how to successfully quit."

James John Hollandsworth, M.D.

"This guidebook makes TOTAL SENSE. Observing those in my family who have successfully quit smoking - and those who have not - Cassius identifies and "hits the nail on the head" as to the exact roadblocks to success."

Judy Herzanek, Changing Lives Foundation

"Positively Quit Manual by Cassius Cheong is like a big gift in a small package. The little book has many nuggets of wisdom. I recommend the book for smokers who want to quit positively."

Neharika Vohra, Ph.D., Social Psych., Professor

"Quitting is a process more than an event, and this little book gives a good overview of the road to a quitter's attitude and a lot of encouragement for the journey.'

Judith Paley M.D.

"The manual provides a step by step approach to preparing to quit, managing smoking triggers, handling the first day and then maintaining progress. It is a complete but concise guide to success with smoking cessation even if your previous efforts have left a bad taste in your mouth."

Dr. Joseph G. Langen

"Check out his book for tips on how to accomplish this goal. You CAN become a non-smoker!"

Ramona L. Bates, M.D.

"I really enjoyed the book, and I know it will be extremely helpful to anyone who smokes! It's simple, engaging and offers important perspectives I have never encountered before."

Lauren Marie Owen, Life Coach

"Positively Quit! is a short but very helpful manual for kicking the habit of smoking. When you are truly ready to quit you will need to take the steps outlined in Positively Quit! If you are ready, get this book and follow the steps."

John Chancellor, Mentor Coach

"We used the manual for the Quitober Challenge 2010. Feedback was upbeat and positive: '*Short and informative*', '*Key to my success*' and '*Extremely useful*'. We will definitely be using the PQ Manual in our next challenge campaign."

Des Sherlock, Founder and CEO, Quitober Challenge

CONTENTS

Introduction

There are so many ways to quit smoking. There's going 'cold turkey', 'cutting down', hypnosis, acupuncture, Zyban®, Chantix®, Nicotine Replacement Therapy (NRT) and many more. Each offers some degree of success, yet no one method guarantees it. It's the same with Positively Quit - the suggestions and ideas work for some smokers but not for others.

Who responds best to Positively Quit? My experience with clients is that it works best for smokers who are *open-minded, rational* and *determined to stop smoking for good.* Positively Quit offers new perspectives about smoking addiction and cessation. Readers should be rational enough to understand these new perspectives. Open-mindedness is important because (as you'll see) some Positively Quit practices and advice go against conventional wisdom. It helps when readers are open enough to accept these new approaches.

Understanding and acceptance facilitate positively quitting. Determination is the third and likely most important quality. Positive Quitters are determined to become non-smokers again. Most have tried quitting numerous times and failed. They embark on Positively Quit determined to succeed.

How can readers get the most from this manual? Here are some suggestions.

First, and most importantly, *read it with an open mind.* My experience, as a smoker looking for effective ways to quit and as someone who helps other smokers quit, is that some conventional smoking cessation guidance and advice is suspect or plain wrong. To make matters worse, the parts that don't work hinder smoking cessation - they make quitting even harder. Be open to the possibility that some 'truths' about cigarette smoking may be false. If you've tried quitting several times and failed (like most other smokers), consider that it may not be your fault that you were not able to quit. You may think or were told you failed because you didn't follow the instructions correctly. Or you may think you failed because you didn't have the willpower. Perhaps you were given the wrong instructions derived from incorrect information and this made staying off cigarettes more difficult than necessary.

Second, please do the recommended exercises. Some of them may seem unusual or feel contrived. Do them anyway. The payoff will be an easier quit so the effort will be well worth it. Moreover, with time and practice, you'll likely find the exercises becoming an integral part of you. By then they'll feel more natural and require little or no effort to do.

Data shows that most smokers who attempt to quit will relapse. Use the information and tools in this manual and you'll likely find yourself succeeding. As you've probably guessed, positively quitting won't be effortless - you'll still have to put in some effort. This is, on the whole, a good thing. If quitting were effortless, what's to stop you from smoking again in the future? So, in this instance, a pinch of pain and some effort quitting is helpful. They'll be your friends - they'll help you remember why you don't want to start smoking again, ever.

On the other hand, you'll likely find it easier to stay off cigarettes compared to say, going cold turkey or cutting down. The tools in this manual will give you leverage so you won't need as much effort or willpower quitting, compared to those methods. Quitting will seem more manageable and less tedious.

Whether you're a rational and open-minded smoker or not, your decision to quit for good is the most important step to ending your cigarette addiction. I hope that, one way or another, you'll find this manual a useful tool to help you stop smoking for good.

Note: Cigarette smoking is recognised as both an addiction as well as a psychological dependence. To avoid confusion, I use the term addiction loosely, to include psychological dependence as well. See answers.com for a good explanation of the differences - http://www.answers.com/topic/addiction.

PART 1

CIGARETTES AND I

Take a few minutes to answer the questions from pages 4 to 6 (please do so before proceeding).

Why I want to stop smoking:

- ☐ I don't want to get lung cancer, emphysema or any other terrible diseases from smoking
- ☐ Present health problems
- ☐ My doctor advised me to quit
- ☐ A family member / friend just died / is dying from a smoking-related disease
- ☐ I'm quitting for a new love in my life
- ☐ I'm quitting for the sake of my partner
- ☐ I am / my wife is pregnant and I don't want to expose the foetus to unnecessary health risks
- ☐ There is a baby in the household now
- ☐ I'm quitting for my kid(s) / grandkid(s)
  - ☐ They don't want me to die from smoking
  - ☐ I want to be a good role model for them
  - ☐ They're already pretending to smoke
- ☐ It's too expensive
- ☐ It's a waste of money
- ☐ Everyone else I know has quit – I'm the only one smoking now
- ☐ Smoking is affecting my sports performance
- ☐ My non-smoker friends and colleagues (even older ones) are much fitter than I am

- ☐ I'm turning ___ & there's not much time left
- ☐ Smoking is too inconvenient – it's banned just about everywhere!
- ☐ Smoking just isn't cool anymore
- ☐ I've grown ashamed of my smoking addiction
- ☐ I've realised how addicted I am to cigarettes
- ☐ I'm tired of sneaking about all day just to smoke
- ☐ I'm tired of feeling dirty and smelly
- ☐ I'm sick of having to smoke this drug every day (and it doesn't even make me high!)
- ☐ I'm tired that cigarettes have more control of my life than I do
- ☐ I feel trapped by my smoking addiction
- ☐ I'm truly tired of *having* to smoke
- ☐ I just feel ready to quit

Other reasons I want to stop smoking:

____

____

____

____

____

____

____

____

Impressions of cigarettes, smoking and quitting

Smokers have varied ideas and opinions about smoking, quitting and about themselves as smokers. Which statements do you agree with?

- ☐ It's easy to pick up smoking
- ☐ Quitting smoking is really difficult
- ☐ Nicotine is the main reason why quitting is so difficult
- ☐ Smoking gives pleasure
- ☐ Smoking helps relieve stress
- ☐ Smoking helps improve concentration
- ☐ I smoke to keep my weight down
- ☐ Cigarettes feel like my good friends
- ☐ I rationalise my smoking addiction and look for examples that smoking is fine e.g. *'My uncle smoked and lived to 90'*
- ☐ Smokers are trendier, more sophisticated, daring, etc. than non-smokers
- ☐ It's frightening to think I'll never smoke ever again
- ☐ I feel trapped by my cigarette addiction
- ☐ I am a light smoker
- ☐ I am a medium smoker
- ☐ I am a heavy smoker

PART 2

A DIFFERENT PERSPECTIVE OF CIGARETTE SMOKING AND ADDICTION

Quitting smoking is really difficult

Let's consider the statements on the previous page, starting with 'Quitting smoking is really difficult'. Did you indicate that it's really tough to stop smoking? The numbers support you if you did.

- Approximately 45.3 million adults in the United States smoke cigarettes.[1]
- 70% report that they want to quit completely.[2]
- 20 million try every year. Only 5% of those who try actually succeed.[3, 4]

Why are success rates so low? I believe the key reason is that most smokers are hardly aware of the powerful psychological aspects of smoking.

Instead, smokers tend to focus on nicotine addiction when quitting. Even after they have resolved their nicotine addiction, many ex-smokers are unaware of the problems caused by their underlying thoughts and feelings about smoking. Those who *are* aware of these detrimental intrusive thoughts and emotions either do not know what to do or simply fail to do anything about them for whatever reasons. The result is

1 *Cigarette Smoking Among Adults, 2006.* Centers for Disease Control and Prevention.

2 *Smoking Cessation Fact Sheet, U.S. Smokers' Attempts to Quit.* Centers for Disease Control and Prevention.

3 *Smoking Cessation: Facing the Challenges of Tobacco Addiction.* Centers for Disease Control and Prevention. August 14, 2001.

4 *Shape of the Relapse Curve and Long-Term Abstinence Among Untreated Smokers.* Hughes JR, Keely J & Naud S. Addiction. January 2004; 99:29-38.

an ex-smoker who is periodically or relentlessly plagued by thoughts and impulses to start smoking again! Quitting is easier when one is able to better manage these unwanted feelings and thoughts.

It's frightening to think I'll never smoke ever again

"You'll never smoke another cigarette for the rest of your life". How would you react if you knew this were true? A minority of smokers might feel relief, but the majority would be horrified. Smokers, by and large, find the thought of never smoking again depressing, bleak and daunting. We may want to stop but, at the same time, we're afraid of missing out on the many 'benefits' of smoking - for pleasure, stress relief, camaraderie etc. We think that, because we're addicted to cigarettes, we'll always have longings for them and will always end up smoking. Not smoking anymore feels like the ultimate deprivation.

Can you imagine yourself:

* letting go of smoking without any regrets?
* not having any doubts or grievances about quitting?
* not missing smoking one bit?

It may seem somewhat of a stretch right now, but this is going to be your new attitude towards smoking and quitting. Achieve this and you'll cope much better during the first few days, weeks and months of not smoking. Cultivating and then embracing this new attitude will help you remain a contented non-smoker for the rest of your life, one who's completely free of cigarettes in every sense of the word.

Before we head there though, let's consider this simple question..

Why start smoking?

If people believe that smoking is harmful, addictive and difficult to stop, why do they start smoking in the first place? People pick up smoking for numerous reasons. These are the more popular ones:

- ☐ Out of curiosity
- ☐ To be cool
- ☐ To be, look or feel rougher and tougher
- ☐ To be more sophisticated
- ☐ To be grown up
- ☐ To be accepted / fit in with my friends
- ☐ To be like my idol
- ☐ Because everyone else was doing it
- ☐ To tick my parents or teachers off
- ☐ I was so angry and upset that I wanted to kill myself
- ☐ My parents / brother / sister smoked

Did you start smoking for any of these reasons? Probably. Are any of these reasons relevant to you now? Unlikely, I'd say. If you didn't already smoke, would you pick it up for any of these reasons? Even more unlikely. This is because the reasons listed above are, for the most part, those given by kids and teenagers - why kids say they take up smoking.

It's helpful to face up to the fact that we took up smoking because *we were young, immature and knew less well.* It is for these reasons that we allowed ourselves to be beguiled by (mostly well-meaning) friends and family members into learning to smoke.

This is also why people smoke for years or decades before even considering quitting. It is after we've grown more mature and have come to accept ourselves for who we are that our original motivations for smoking become irrelevant.

What about you? Aren't there things you used to do in your youth that seemed appropriate and fun, but are now simply silly, inappropriate or embarrassing? Wouldn't smoking be one of those things? Picking up smoking seemed fun and exciting when we were young, but with experience and repetition, it gets irrelevant and tiresome. Like all the other things that you've outgrown and happily discarded, why not let go of cigarette smoking as well.

Smoking relieves stress, gives pleasure & improves concentration

Did you indicate that smoking helps relieve stress? That it gives you pleasure or helps you concentrate? Most smokers identify with at least one of these statements. These three beliefs are interrelated. Each is tied to the fact that the smoker is addicted to cigarettes. Because of our nicotine addiction, we experience tension and discomfort whenever the nicotine level in our blood falls below a level we've grown accustomed to. We are distracted and have trouble focusing.

We habitually feel like smoking whenever this happens. By smoking, we raise the nicotine level in our blood. This relieves the tension and we feel better. We can then get back to living our lives – at least for a while. The problem is that most of us are unaware that this is happening. Instead, we're duped into thinking that smoking helps to relieve stress, gives pleasure and improves concentration.

Smoking helps relieve stress

Many smokers say they smoke to alleviate stress. The truth, though, is that smoking causes more stress than it relieves. Smoking frequently develops into an addiction. This addiction causes stress-like symptoms - tension, irritability and anxiety - when we don't smoke. Smoking allays these symptoms and we're fooled into thinking it relieves stress!

Psychologist Andy Parrott, Ph.D., reviewed studies on the smoking/stress relationship, first in adult smokers, then in novice adolescent smokers and lastly during smoking cessation. He found that, instead of helping improve one's mood, nicotine dependency *tends to increase stress.*[1] Professor Parrott concluded: "The repeated occurrence of negative moods between cigarettes means that smokers tend to experience slightly above-average levels of daily stress. Thus, nicotine dependency seems to be a direct cause of stress."

Some studies showed that former smokers were less stressed than current smokers. It seems the ex-smoker has one less source of stress when the addiction is cured.

Smoking produces other stresses, of course. We worry we might get lung cancer or other protracted smoking-related diseases, followed by a slow and painful death. Many smokers are periodically nagged by well-meaning spouses, pestered by their worried kids or even harassed by their companies to quit smoking. Probably the biggest pain about smoking is that we're as good as chained to our packets of cigarettes. We're constantly concerned we'll run out or won't be able to smoke. Running out of cigarettes (and then not being able to buy any) is a big hassle. So is being stuck in a place where we

[1] *Does Cigarette Smoking Cause Stress?* Andy C. Parrott, University of East London.

can't smoke. These niggling worries lay dormant when all's going well, but as smokers, we know they're always at the back of our minds.

Stop smoking long enough and all these concerns will disappear. *You'll experience less stress and feel freer* when this happens.

Smoking helps improve concentration

Smokers commonly believe that smoking helps improve concentration. In the case of the addicted smoker though, most of this improvement comes from the relief of withdrawal symptoms. Nicotine withdrawal creates problems that distract us and make concentrating difficult. Smoking relieves nicotine withdrawal allowing us to focus on the task at hand. We end up believing smoking improves our concentration when it is our addiction that is making it difficult for us to concentrate in the first place! Even worse, we suffer from these mini-withdrawal symptoms many times every day. Every time it happens, we have to light up to feed our addiction. Each time we do not, we're distracted by an irksome void - diminishing our capacity to focus and deal with issues at hand.

Smoking gives pleasure

Smokers look forward to their smokes. Each cigarette is a little treat as we go through the day. The cigarettes with our coffee, after lunch, during breaks and before bed are all little treats we look forward to throughout the day. Sometimes these little treats act as rewards for completing tasks or activities.

Yet, there's a problem with the nature of these treats. They are borne of our nicotine addiction. Our bodies need a constant level of nicotine throughout the day because of this addiction. Otherwise, we suffer mini-withdrawal symptoms.

We all look forward to our first cigarette of the day. The amount of nicotine in our blood is at its lowest when we wake up (our bodies continually clear and metabolise nicotine, even when we're sleeping). That's why the first cigarette of the day feels especially good – *your addiction is craving for nicotine*. Smoking satisfies this craving. Feeling good and 'pleasure' is how your addicted body rewards you for satisfying its addiction. Not long afterwards, you'll experience another bout of mini-withdrawal symptoms. You need to smoke another cigarette to alleviate them, otherwise you can't function normally.

Your body goes through this cycle many times throughout the day. This is the nature of our treats (and the illusion that smoking gives pleasure): We created an addiction to nicotine when we learned to smoke. What we think is pleasure is actually tension relief. By not smoking, our addicted bodies rapidly build up a craving for cigarettes. Smoking relieves the tension and is translated as 'pleasure' by the deprived smoker.

If you're reading this book, it likely means you can't stop smoking - you're addicted to it. Rather than relieving stress, providing pleasure or improving concentration, your cigarette addiction is *hindering* concentration and producing *even more* stress! Imagine life without cigarettes - you'll be rid of an annoying addiction, experience less stress and feel freer on the whole.

I smoke to keep my weight down

Smoking does suppress appetite and hunger signals. An improved appetite is often a side effect when one stops smoking. Furthermore, some quitters use food as a cigarette substitute or for emotional comfort. As a result, older smokers tend to put on some 2 to 4 kg (5 to 10 lbs) after quitting. However, there are lots of ways to keep your weight down. If your diet remains unchanged after you've stopped smoking, you can shed the gain by taking a brisk 30-minute walk daily. The exercise will also improve your mood.

Focus on staying off cigarettes, not your weight. If you do gain some weight after quitting, resist the urge to smoke again. Live with the weight gain for a while and stay focused on not smoking. Experiment with different ways to lose the weight you gained only when you feel confident you are able to stay off cigarettes.

Cigarettes feel like my good friends

Do you think of cigarettes as your 'good friends'? Some smokers do. This is not surprising considering these smokers think their cigarettes keep them company when they're alone, relieve stress, help keep them trim and project the correct image. Another reason is that smokers have had cigarettes by their side for years or decades. Most smokers can hardly remember a time when they didn't have cigarettes by their side.

The truth, of course, is that the cigarette is nothing more than an addictive tobacco product that big tobacco companies have spent billions improving and marketing.

If you still feel that the cigarette is your friend, consider that cigarettes have always been *phoney* friends. We've all had those. They were the people who told us they were our friends but said cruel things about us behind our backs. They were the ones who used us to make themselves look good. Their main intention was to exploit us for their own selfish gains.

Are cigarettes much different?

They've appeared to comfort and be there for you. The truth is, like false friends, they're secretly working behind your back. They're trying to get you sick. They're constantly trying to control and manipulate you - to take away your enjoyment of life. All these years they've been with you, they've been slowly sucking the very life out of you.

Sometimes it may seem difficult to let even bad 'friends' go. You may have enjoyed times with your cigarettes, but you know it's all for the best to simply let them go. Later on, like many other things you've reluctantly let go of, you'll look back and be happy with the choice you made.

I rationalise my smoking addiction

Who among us doesn't rationalise our smoking addiction? We tell ourselves:

"I am a light smoker so I'm safe"

"My grandmother smoked and lived to 86"

"I smoke light cigarettes which cause much less harm"

At the same time, we do our best to minimise in our minds, the likelihood we'll contract a terrible tobacco-induced illness.

We know our rationalisations are simply part of a strategy we use to comfort ourselves. We rationalise cigarette smoking to make it appear safe (despite knowing otherwise). We do this so that we can continue smoking with some peace of mind. Why not face up to the truth about your smoking addiction once and for all? You know that cigarette smoking is wasteful and harmful. Resolve to stop for good.

Ask ex-smokers (anyone who's stopped for more than a year) how they feel about not smoking. You'll find the overwhelming response is that they're glad they managed to quit. Most feel more confident and pleased with themselves for quitting. You'll be glad and pleased with yourself too when you've rid yourself of this wearisome addiction.

Smokers are trendier, more sophisticated, daring, etc. than non-smokers

Are smokers trendier, more sophisticated and daring than non-smokers? Lots of smokers like to think so. Do you? I certainly did. Lots of us started smoking for the imagery or look, for example, to look cool, appear tough and grown up. To many smokers - especially younger ones - smoking is like wearing a big badge. They smoke trying to project those qualities they associate with smoking.

If you believe smoking somehow improves your image, if you think smokers are trendier or more sophisticated, you're going to find quitting disagreeable. You're likely to worry that you'll somehow have less of these qualities if you stop smoking. Put your worries to rest. Look at the following traits:

Tense
Anxious
Depressive
Impulsive
Neurotic
Sensation seeking
Novelty seeking
Non-conventional
Hostile
Anti-social
Likely to show mood disorder symptoms

What do you think of these characteristics? What's your impression of someone who is characterised by three or more of these traits? Weak? Confused? Pitiful? Years of scientific research show that smokers in general tend to score *higher* on these attributes compared to non-smokers.[1] Therefore, the truth is that smokers are *not* cooler, trendier or more sophisticated. Instead, they are generally more anxious, depressive, tense and neurotic than non-smokers.

Let's face it – we started smoking because we were young and insecure. We smoked hoping to feel stronger and more confident. We smoked to look rougher and tougher, to win the approval of our smoking friends. We smoked to belong. It was the right thing to do, based on what we knew then. Now we're more mature, more centred and don't need to smoke to look cool or belong. The natural thing to do is to let our cigarette smoking go.

I feel trapped by my cigarette addiction

Have you ever felt trapped by your tobacco dependency? If you have, you're probably not alone. Most smokers try stopping several times, trying one method after another, but are still unable to quit. If this happens to someone often enough, he may develop 'learned helplessness' to his smoking problem and resign himself to be a 'confirmed smoker'. This self-perception would be further reinforced if he reads or is told that smoking *is* remarkably difficult to quit, due to nicotine's highly addictive nature.

1 See studies referred to in *A Comparative Study of Personality Traits in College Undergraduate Smokers, Ex-Smokers and Non-Smokers.* Regina de Cássia Rondina, Ricardo Gorayeb, Clóvis Botelho and Ageo Mário Cândido da Silva. Universidade de São Paulo.

Ability belief. Do you believe you can quit smoking? If not, you won't be able to. To do anything, each of us must first believe on some level we can do it.

The good news is ability belief can be influenced and changed. For instance, suppose Melanie, a long time smoker, believes she can't stop smoking. She 'needs' to smoke at least 40 cigarettes a day. One day, Melanie discovers that a friend she has drinks with recently quit smoking. This friend was an even heavier smoker than Melanie and seemed even more dependent on cigarettes. Now, not only has she quit, she's going on with her life as if nothing's happened. Seeing this would quite likely change Melanie's own ability belief about quitting. In fact, it would dramatically influence Melanie's belief that it could be done and that she could do it.

Exercise: Draw up a list of your personal achievements on the next page (create your own table if this one's not large enough). These accomplishments could be anything that you invested a significant amount of time and effort learning or achieving. Or they could simply be anything you're proud of. Add 'Overcame smoking addiction', as the newest item, in the last row. For example:

Won spelling bee (1974)

Karate, brown belt (1980)

Got my first promotion (1987)

Doing good job raising great kids - Elliot and Emma

Overcame smoking addiction!!

My Accomplishments

❄ ❄ ❄ ❄ ❄

KNOW THAT YOU'LL ACCOMPLISH THIS TOO AND LOOK FORWARD TO IT!

❄ ❄ ❄ ❄ ❄

Brace yourself for this achievement. There's absolutely no reason why you can't do it. *Tens of millions* of smokers - many of whom smoked as much as, if not more than you - have stopped for good. And the majority did so without any special aids or tools.

It's easy to pick up smoking

Did you indicate that it's easy to pick up smoking? Smokers have different experiences with their first cigarettes. If you smoked a 'modern cigarette', learning to smoke would be considerably easier than with an older, more traditionally manufactured cigarette. This is because modern cigarettes tend to be smoother and easier to learn to smoke. Cigarette makers add sweeteners to cigarettes to enhance the taste of tobacco smoke, thereby increasing their cigarettes' appeal, especially to starting adolescent smokers. Some cigarettes have eugenol and menthol to numb the throat against tobacco smoke's aggravating effects.

What was smoking *your* first cigarette like? If you smoked a middle- to high-tar cigarette, the weakly filtered, noxious chemicals in the smoke likely had a nasty impact on you,* producing one or more of the following reactions:

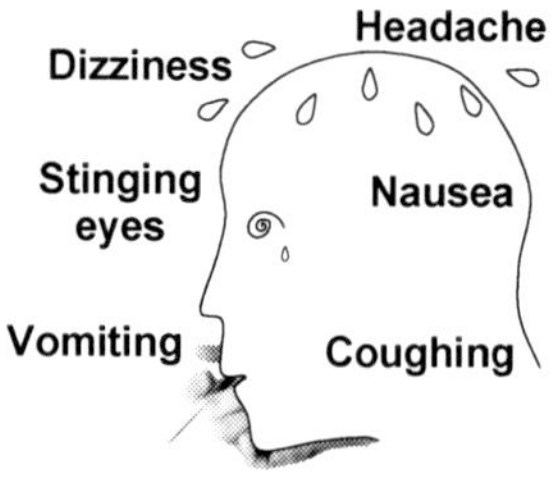

These were our bodies' distress signals. Our bodies were *crying for us to stop*, but we carried on. Many did stop and remained non-smokers. We persisted in becoming smokers. We forced our bodies to get used to

* Although we're discussing those among us who had difficulty learning to smoke, there's a lesson here for all of us in quitting.

the tar, nicotine and other toxins in the cigarette smoke.

Why did we keep smoking if it was so painful? We did so, and were able to, because *we were highly motivated to!* You don't buy this? It's corroborated by Big Tobacco's own research:

> For the pre-smoker and "learner" the physical effects of smoking are largely unknown, unneeded or actually quite unpleasant or awkward* [i.e. the physical effects of cigarette smoke make learning to smoke difficult]. The expected or derived psychological effects [i.e. the desired image as a smoker] are largely responsible for influencing the pre-smoker to try smoking, and provide sufficient motivation during the "learning" period to keep the "learner" going, despite the physical unpleasantness and awkwardness of the period.[1]

So in the beginning, we coped and dealt with all the unpleasantness because we were feeling adventurous, happy and excited that we were becoming smokers! What can we learn from this? Wanting something badly, approaching it with enthusiasm and delight, makes all the difference in achieving it. That's how you and your friends succeeded in becoming smokers despite the initial disgust and unpleasantness. Likewise, getting ourselves off cigarettes for good also becomes easier when we are excited and enthusiastic about it. The problem is that smokers approach it the other way around: Nearly all smokers approach quitting with dread and fear. The thought of never being able to smoke again horrifies them. No wonder the vast majority fails!

* Even Big Tobacco knew then that ***cigarette smoking isn't pleasurable.*** Instead, the 'physical effects of smoking are largely unknown, unneeded, unpleasant or awkward' to the not-yet-addicted person! This person has to be sufficiently motivated to keep going, 'despite the physical unpleasantness and awkwardness', simply to learn to smoke. *There's clearly no pleasure here!*

1 *Some Thoughts about New Brands of Cigarettes for the Youth Market.* February 2, 1973, RJR memo.

* * * * *

APPROACH BECOMING A NON-SMOKER AGAIN WITH A SENSE OF ADVENTURE, ENTHUSIASM AND EXCITEMENT.

DO THIS AND YOU WILL FIND QUITTING MUCH EASIER.

* * * * *

All fired up: Then and Now

Then: Eager and excited to become a smoker	**Now: Eager and excited to be a *non-smoker* again**
I wonder what it feels like to smoke?	I wonder what it's like not having to smoke anymore?
Ah! So this is what smoking is like!	Ah! So this is what it's like not having to smoke!
Cool! I'm smoking!	Nice! I'm able to stay off cigarettes!
I'll keep smoking until I stop coughing, feeling ill, until my eyes stop watering, etc.	I've stopped – I'm done with smoking for good!
People are going to show me more respect.	I don't really care what other people think.
I carry smokes around with me - like a real smoker!	It'll be interesting not being chained to a pack of cigarettes anymore!
It took some time to get the hang of it, but I'm a real smoker now!	I've made several attempts to stop smoking – this time I'm going to do it!

Exercise: Think of an occasion when you felt really good about yourself. Experience it again - the place, the sights, sounds, smells and especially your feelings. Close your eyes and relive the moment. Enjoy it. Now imagine you're in the future - you *know* you're free of cigarettes and feel exactly the same way. **You've beaten your cigarette dependency hands down and feel great!** Do this every now and then until you've stopped smoking.

Nicotine

Did you indicate that nicotine is the main reason quitting is so difficult? We've all read or heard that nicotine is very addictive, even more addictive than crack cocaine or heroin. Nicotine - like cocaine, heroin and methamphetamine - produces a rapid spike in dopamine, a chemical that causes feelings of reward and pleasure. That's why it's so addictive.

But is nicotine really more addictive than crack cocaine and the other drugs it's compared with? Some simple, everyday observations suggest otherwise. For example:

Not everyone is easily addicted to tobacco smoke (in spite of nicotine's addictiveness): We saw earlier that, even in 1973, executives at RJ Reynolds knew that smoking is not something that comes naturally or is easy to do. One needs to *learn* how to do it. Learning to smoke can be very awkward and disagreeable. In fact, it can be so awkward and unpleasant that many beginners need to be sufficiently motivated to learn to smoke. Otherwise they give up trying.

A study commissioned by Imperial Tobacco, found that cigarettes 'were just too harsh and irritating and caused symptoms Experimenter/Rejectors were not prepared to endure'. In other words, the nicotine in cigarettes isn't so addictive that anyone trying one can't resist wanting more. Instead, many find tobacco smoke *repulsive.*

Smokers routinely control their nicotine cravings despite their addiction:

- Many smokers occasionally 'forget' to smoke, especially when pleasantly distracted. Examples include when watching a movie or experiencing 'flow' while working.
- During Ramadan, most Pakistani Muslim smokers (76% to 92%) stop smoking during their fast. [1, 2]
- Smokers don't run amok from not being able to smoke on long-haul flights. They don't need NRT gum or patches either. Smokers are able to cope so well that we're not able to identify smokers (from non-smokers) among our fellow passengers simply by looking at them.
- When warded in hospital, *all* smokers can go without smoking. Here again, the effects of not being able to smoke are not so bad that the smoker has to be restrained. He may feel uncomfortable, but he can control his urge to smoke.

The majority of smokers successfully quit without NRT or other pharmaceutical aids: Dr. Simon Chapman and Ross Mackenzie reviewed 511 studies published in 2007 and 2008. They determined that "Up to three-quarters of ex-smokers have quit without assistance ('cold turkey' or cut

1 *Comparison of Population Survey of Multan About Cigarette Smoking with Survey of Abbottabad.* Muhammad Asif Jaleel, Rozina Nooreen, Abida Parveen, Farhana, Nadeem and Abdul Hameed. Journal of Ayub Med Coll Abbottabad. Jan - Mar 2002; 14(1) pp 16-19.

2 *Barriers to Smoking Cessation: Results of a Survey Among Family Practice Patients.* Dr. Waris Qidwai, Associate Professor, Family Medicine, The Aga Khan University. Middle East Journal of Family Medicine, 2004; Vol. 5 (5)

down then quit)."[1] They also reported "more smokers find it unexpectedly easy or moderately difficult than find it very difficult to quit". They concluded that "A serious attempt at stopping need not involve using NRT or other drugs or getting professional support."

Now consider your own tobacco addiction - does it feel like you're hooked on heroin or crack cocaine? Are you so preoccupied with smoking that it's overtaken your life? Are you forsaking your family relationships, friendships, children, food and sex because you need to smoke? Or do you choose to not smoke occasionally? You might get irritable, cranky and have difficulty concentrating if you're not able to smoke when you want to. Despite this, isn't it more correct to say that you are *not* under nicotine's control? Don't *you* remain in control? You can choose to rant and rave or you can choose to stay calm and in charge. You could stop smoking using pharmaceutical aids but you'd likely do fine without them. Like the majority of ex-smokers before you, you might find quitting unexpectedly easy or only moderately difficult.

What if nicotine has a stronger hold upon you, one you find unmanageable? What if you've already decided you're going to use medical aids to help you stop? Two reminders if you're taking this route: First, use the medication as directed. Second, keep in mind that these medications are *aids* to help you stop smoking. They won't make you stop. You'll have to want to. You'll also have to take an active role in the process. Use the exercises and tools in this manual to help you.

* * * * *

1 *The Global Research Neglect of Unassisted Smoking Cessation: Causes and Consequences.* Simon Chapman & Ross MacKenzie, PLoS Medicine, February 2010; Vol. 7 (2).

PART 3
QUIT PREPARATIONS

Set a day to quit not later than one week from today. Carry on smoking until then.

Become aware of your triggers

Ivan Pavlov conducted a series of experiments in the 1890s that made history. Pavlov rang a metronome at the same time he gave his dogs food. He noticed that, over time, the dogs would start to salivate when the metronome sounded, even when no food was present. He called this learning process conditioning. Pavlov found that conditioning could be unlearned. If the metronome sounds repeatedly and no food materialises, eventually the dogs stop salivating to the sound.

How does this relate to smoking? If you smoke each time you have coffee, you're going to condition yourself to expect a cigarette when you have a cuppa. If you regularly smoke at a particular stairwell in your office building, you'll condition yourself to expect a smoke each time you're in that stairwell. Do you drive and smoke? Then getting behind the wheel will likely trigger an urge to smoke.

In smoking cessation, the coffee, stairwell and act of getting behind the wheel of a car are examples of what we call *triggers*. They trigger the expectation and want of a cigarette. Start noticing what your own triggers are likely to be. When you've identified them, imagine yourself not smoking in the presence of your triggers. If coffee is a trigger for you, have your cups of coffee imagining how interesting and unusual it'll feel having coffee without cigarettes. Get used to the idea and sense of not smoking to your triggers.

Experiment not smoking to fill in 'dull' time

Some smokers feel the urge to light up whenever they're waiting. Sometimes it's because they're bored. At other times it's because they feel self-conscious. They're afraid someone might look at them and wonder why they're there, alone and doing nothing. They feel awkward.

Is this true for you? Whatever the reason, if you tend to light up to fill in free time or when waiting for something or someone, practice undoing it. Say you're standing somewhere, waiting for someone. Try *not* lighting up a cigarette. Simply stand there or stroll around at a leisurely pace. Don't fold your arms or put them into your trouser pockets. Just let your arms hang by your sides, relaxed.

Likewise, try not smoking while sitting somewhere waiting. Resist getting something to eat or drink either. Just sit there with your arms at your side, hands resting on your lap or on your seat. Relax. Look around you. Slowly take in whatever's happening in the vicinity while you wait.

Start being more productive with your time. Commit yourself to doing things that are going to make life better. You could spend the extra time you have not smoking to catch up on little things that need to be done.

Quit for someone else

Some smokers remind themselves that their health will improve. Others keep track of how much money they're saving by not smoking. The focus is inward in each case -

directed towards the smoker. This is the thrust of most smoking cessation strategies - to focus on the benefits the smoker derives from quitting.

If quitting for yourself (to save money, improve your health or social status) didn't work in the past, you might want to try *not smoking for someone else.* For instance, many smokers quit when expecting a baby or when they have small kids. I'm one of them. We do so because we want what's best for them. Quitting's a very good idea because of first- and second-hand smoke. Furthermore, kids tend to pick up smoking if they live in a home where an adult smokes.

Who should we stop smoking for? Choose someone or something that (1) you love dearly and (2) has little chance of upsetting you considerably (so much that you're not able to get over it quickly). The second criterion is important because, if you do quit for someone, and if this person upsets you enough, you might consider the sacrifice a waste of your effort and start smoking again. Appropriate people or things include babies, young children, your favourite dog or cat or a memory of someone dear, especially someone who'd have been glad you quit. If you're a religious person, you might even consider quitting for God.

Are you pregnant? Your foetus or baby is completely defenceless and at your mercy. Smoking exposes it to many health risks and potential complications. *Think about how much better off baby would be if you didn't smoke.* Haven't you already made sacrifices for baby? You may have adjusted your diet; you may be channelling more time or money from yourself towards baby. Why not stop smoking as well? Consider it one more sacrifice you'll be willing to make for it.

Do you have small kids? If you do, one or more of them is likely to have pleaded with you not to smoke. Your kids are dependent on you. They need you. If you're like most parents, you'll have sacrificed sleep, money, some personal freedom and more for them. You've already given up so much for them. Why not stop smoking for them as well? Let this be just one more sacrifice you'll be happy to make for your kids.

Are you religious? If you are, do you think God approves, is indifferent to, or disapproves of you smoking? If you believe God would want you to not smoke, consider quitting for God. If you're Christian, take it a step further - If Jesus Christ were willing to die on a cross for you, could you make one sacrifice for him - by not smoking? It's a small sacrifice in comparison, and you'll be living your life as you've always, with the exception of not smoking anymore.

Exercise: Do the following each time the occasion arises. Keep going until you have your last cigarette. The more second nature they become, the easier it'll be to stay smoke free.

Quietly feel sorry for the smokers around you

- You know they're smoking to satisfy their addicted bodies' nicotine craving.
- They're unable to stay focused for long without a smoke because of this addiction.
- They feel like smoking every time they're under pressure. If they can't smoke, they end up feeling even more stressed.
- They probably don't know they have this problem to begin with. Instead, they think their cigarette is their friend!
- Look at the guy with his hand out of the car window, holding a cigarette as he's driving. He thinks doing so shows

he's unrestrained and cool. The truth is he's likely to have tried quitting more than once but failed to each time. He'll likely continue being chained to his packets of cigarettes for years to come.

* Remember - **be confident and believe you'll succeed!** This will have a big impact on the outcome. You may have had problems quitting in the past. You may have had doubts about your own ability to quit before reading this manual. Know and look forward to the fact that you're going to succeed this time!
* Keep in mind that your attitude towards quitting will impact how easy or difficult it will be. Approach quitting with dread and trepidation? Be prepared for a rough ride. Go into your quit with eagerness and anticipation and it'll likely be easier than you'd expected.

Look forward to becoming a non-smoker again

* 'Not being able to smoke will no longer affect me when I'm celebrating and enjoying myself. Smokers, on the other hand, can't enjoy themselves as much if they run out of cigarettes or aren't allowed to smoke.'
* 'I won't have to leave the building or look for stairwells to smoke in anymore.'
* 'Worrying if I have enough cigarettes with me will be a thing of the past.'
* 'My health will improve.'
* 'My complexion will improve and I'll be more attractive' (women know and care that smoking causes premature skin ageing and wrinkling).

- 'If I decide to quit for the kids, I anticipate how they'll see me in a new light. I know that by not smoking, my kids are going to be much less likely to take it up. If they do pick up smoking, they're unlikely to listen to me to stop if I'm still smoking. So - because I know that smoking is rubbish - I'm glad I'm quitting for their sake.'
- 'I know that there's so much more to me than just someone who smokes. Being a smoker is just one small part of me. I've loads of skills and abilities, relationships, achievements, passions, fond memories and more. After I've let smoking go, *I'll still have everything that really matters in my life.*'
- 'I visualise myself as a non-smoker happily living life.'
- 'I'm at ease with myself and feel completely liberated.'

Goal #1

You will achieve two key goals in your Positive Quit. Your first goal is to **stay off cigarettes for at least 24 hours**. Here's why - the Fred Hutchinson Cancer Research Center found that:

> "Smokers who successfully shun cigarettes during the first 24 hours of a quit attempt are 10 times more likely to kick the habit permanently than those unable to stay smokeless for a day."[1]

Just succeeding here improves your chances of quitting for good by 1000%! Have you succeeded in not smoking for more than 24 hours during one or more past quit attempts? If you have, don't worry that you started smoking again. It's good that you managed to stay off cigarettes for more than

1 *Trying to quit cigarettes? Hutch researcher offers tips for keeping one's willpower from going up in smoke.* See www.fhcrc.org/about/ne/news/1999/11/12/Smokeout99.html

a day - this shows that you have a pretty good hold on your addiction. Stick with the plan here and you should find it easier to complete Goal #2 and quitting in general.

Plan to have your last cigarette before bed

Suppose your quit day is Saturday and you smoke your last cigarette on Saturday morning. This creates a problem: You've just recharged your addiction with a nicotine fix. Your addicted body will now expect another cigarette, sooner than later. You'll now have the rest of your waking day to think about not smoking. And by bedtime, you'll still not have completed your first goal.

On the other hand, suppose you have your last cigarette on Saturday night. This will probably be in tune with your regular smoking behaviour (of having your last cigarette of the day before going to sleep). When you get up in the morning, you'll be about eight hours into your first 24 hours of quitting. Then you'll spend 16 hours steadying yourself into the life of a non-smoker again.

By the time you get to bed, you'll have accomplished your first goal and will be 10 times more likely to stop smoking for good! Achieve this and you'll go to sleep feeling great about yourself.

Mini-Goals

Feel free to add mini-goals of your own until you achieve Goal #2 (next). For example, you may want to set personal goals to stay off cigarettes for a week, and then a month and so on. Go ahead and set mini-goals that feel right for you.

Goal #2

Let's suppose that what is true for smokers in America is true for smokers elsewhere in the world. We saw on page 7 that about half of the smokers there try to quit every year. Out of every 100 smokers who do try, only five succeed. Your next key goal is to **be among the five percent that stops smoking for good.** You are going to succeed and beat the other 95 percent who are not going to make it.* You have the know-how and tools to help you. All you need is some motivation and the belief you can do it. The best part is that - like everything else in life - it may be a little difficult at first, but it gets easier and easier over time.

Give yourself enough time and you won't even think of smoking anymore.

❄ ❄ ❄ ❄ ❄

* Some people don't want to vie for the top five spaces. That's fine. If you're one of them, ignore this and simply *focus on staying a non-smoker for more than a year.*

PART 4
POSITIVELY QUITTING

It's the evening of your quit. Save one cigarette - and something to light it with - for your last smoke. Crush and throw the rest away. Don't think this a waste. Definitely do not give them to someone else. Throw everything related to smoking - ashtrays, matches and lighters - away. Do not dispose of them in a waste paper basket where they can be retrieved and reused. Dump them in a public bin instead. Smoke your last cigarette and then trash the lighter or matches.

At this point, you may or may not feel profoundly sad and depressed - like your best friend just died or that you've suddenly lost a part of yourself. You may find it difficult to reconcile with the idea of not being able to smoke any longer. You may have second thoughts about whether or not to call the quit off. You may feel like going down to the shop to buy another packet of cigarettes. Some smokers experience these thoughts and feelings when quitting. Others do not. Bear with them, should they happen to you. Give yourself a treat of chocolate, ice cream or some other comfort food (just this once if you're concerned about your weight). Stay away from alcohol. Go to bed knowing these unpleasant feelings and thoughts will eventually go away.

Feel good about yourself for having the courage to take the first step. You're on your way now! Know and feel happy that you're going to make it!

Staying a non-smoker

If you quit the previous night, wake up with your eye on the ball. You're a third of the way through your first goal. Look forward to achieving it.

Your new life as an ex-smoker may seem a little surreal. You may feel somewhat unsteady and unsure. If you do feel this way, it's because you're suddenly out of your old groove. You have an entrenched smoking routine that you moulded through years of repetition. That's okay. And don't worry. You'll gradually get undone from your old smoking patterns and settle into a new non-smoker routine within a week or two.

*** * * Important * * ***

Remember, you're a non-smoker now; **don't do things that non-smokers wouldn't do**. For example, someone may advise you to buy a new pack of cigarettes and keep it somewhere out of sight at home. Your well-meaning friend tells you that doing this will make you proud of yourself for not smoking. Don't do it. Non-smokers don't have packets of cigarettes lying around the house, neither should you. You're a non-smoker and have nothing to do with cigarettes - period.

Don't kick up a fuss. Be the epitome of cool on the first days of your quit. Don't kick up a fuss about anything, especially about withdrawal symptoms or about quitting.

Here's a lesson to learn from: Norman Zinberg and John Robertson observed that heroin addicts at the Daytop Village are expected to carry on with life and are not excused from work duties even when they show withdrawal symptoms. As a result, they do not show many withdrawal symptoms. Many of the same patients went through extreme withdrawal in prison where such behaviour was expected.

It works the same when we're quitting cigarettes. When we create a fuss, things related to the quit tend to get amplified, such as the voices in our heads telling us how uncomfortable and unbearable not smoking is. What we want when quitting is just the opposite - behaving like it's just another day, and quitting is just a small part of that day. So don't make a fuss.* Doing so will only exacerbate things.

Keeping the pressure up

You're likely to have read elsewhere that one should go public before quitting. Doing so puts more pressure on us to succeed. If we're lucky we'll have friends and family members pitching in to give us support. If you think this would help and if you're comfortable with the attention, then go public! You should be aware though, that talking just a little too much about quitting and going on about how we're going to succeed can have a *negative* effect. We tell our friends, family and colleagues that we're quitting, that we're excited about it and know we'll make it. We start feeling good about our 'progress' even though, at this point, we have not achieved anything yet. The problem is that this false sense of accomplishment can relieve 'internal pressure' so that we may not take the quit as seriously as we would otherwise. Let this happen and you'll increase your chances of slipping and failing.

* Easier said than done I know, especially during the first few days. Do your best anyway - it'll be well worth it.

How do we avert this? First, we quit with anticipation and excitement. At the same time, **we keep the pressure up and stay focused on achieving our goals**. At this stage of our quit, we apply ourselves to make Goal #1 - not smoking for at least 24 hours - happen.* When you've done this, you'll have achieved something real and significant (rather than simply imagining it) and it'll be a strong motivator to carry on to achieve your next mini-goal or Goal #2. Meanwhile, if friends or colleagues ask you out for a smoke during your first day, tell them you're busy or that you just don't feel like it.

Online smoking cessation support groups

Should you sign up for one or more online quit smoking support groups? Well, it depends. Are you the kind of person who likes to share (or at least doesn't mind sharing) his quitting experience with others? Many smokers I've worked with would rather not. They see quitting as a private affair. They just want to get it over with, and the less talk about the whole affair the better. At the other end of the scale are smokers who *do* want to talk about it. They want to connect with other smokers who are quitting. They want to share their own quitting experiences. Some say they don't feel so alone when quitting with others. Others find it comforting to get in touch with other newbie ex-smokers so that they can all suffer together in the same boat! Therefore, these support groups can be a great help if they fit your own needs and preferences.

I participated in eight online quit smoking forums for a

* You might want to go public about your quit a day after achieving Goal #1. Do this, stay focused and you'll avoid the problems discuss in this section.

few months in 2010 to get a feel of what they are like. I believe I would have benefited significantly had I done so when I stopped smoking in 2004.

The good: The better forums were active and had a good buzz about them. A few had a strong sense of community and camaraderie. Most importantly, the better forums had members that were, by and large, friendly, helpful and supportive. Post something and you can expect one or more encouraging replies. This support may help get you through difficult periods. If you manage to develop bonds within the group, the sense of belonging will help you feel glad you're a non-smoker again.

Below is a list of some of the online quit smoking forums I had good experiences with. I can't guarantee you'll encounter the same positive experiences but it might be worth your while to dip a toe in to see if the water's right.

Recommended online quit smoking forums

Forum	URL
About.com - Smoking cessation	forums.about.com/n/pfx/forum.aspx?webtag=ab-quitsmoking
Daily Strength's Smoking Addiction & Recovery Support Group	www.dailystrength.org/c/Smoking-Addiction/support-group
No Smoking Day	www.nosmokingday.org.uk/forum/
QuitSmokingMessageBoard.com	www.quitsmokingmessageboard.com
www.soberrecovery.com	www.soberrecovery.com/forums/nicotine-smoking/

The Not-So-Good: Are there downsides to taking part in these forums? Sure. You'll occasionally come across statements and advice that are, in my opinion, not very helpful. They make quitting more difficult.

For instance:

> 'Draw up a list of what you like and dislike about smoking. If your 'like' list is longer than your 'dislike' list, it may not be time for you to quit. You need to think of more reasons to quit'.

(I don't think this piece of advice is particularly helpful because making a list of what one likes about smoking only serves to increase ambivalence about quitting. Uncertainty, hence less resolve, makes staying off cigarettes more difficult.)

Second, you'll come across negative sentiment about quitting. This is commonplace on these forums. I believe these negative statements are a bigger problem than getting poor advice. Some members go on and on about how they love and miss smoking, how they're kicking and screaming because they have to stop, how they keep thinking of cigarettes and so on. Being exposed to such discouraging views may jeopardise your own quit. You may start to question if you too will miss smoking. You may begin to wonder if you'll be able to stop altogether or whether you should just keep on smoking!

Using online quit smoking forums

- If you've not already done so, try joining one or more smoking cessation support groups. Post a short and sweet introduction, then wait and see if you like the responses you get.
- If you decide to participate more, don't feel you need to be an open book up front. You may want to share little bits of yourself at a time instead.
- Be wary of quit smoking ideas and advice you come across or receive.

* Be supportive. Try helping others along. You may find that doing so helps you become stronger in your resolve to stay a non-smoker.
* At the same time, it's probably in your best interest to stay clear of members who go on about how terrible not being able to smoke feels. Let the more experienced ex-smokers - those who have been off cigarettes for months or years - help them. It may seem selfish, but you have to *stay focused on reaching your own goals* first.
* Finally, these forums are simply tools to help you quit. Don't be too reliant on them. Everything you need to stay a non-smoker is within you!

Coffee and caffeine

Approach coffee with caution. Is it likely to be a trigger? If it is, ease into it. Enjoy your coffee thinking how novel it feels drinking coffee without smoking at the same time.

One study showed that people who quit smoking but continued drinking the same amount of coffee had caffeine concentrations in their blood about double the levels before quitting.[1] The same study found that those people who were able to keep to moderate levels of caffeine consumption after quitting suffered from headaches, lethargy, muscle pain, stiffness and mood swings during the process. However, many ex-smokers will tell you that drinking *more* coffee helped them cope with nicotine withdrawal perfectly! Who do we believe?

Experiment going without coffee for a day or two before

[1] *The Impact of Caffeine Use on Tobacco Cessation and Withdrawal.* Swanson JA, Lee JW, Hopp JW, Berk LS. Addictive behaviors. 1997 Jan-Feb;22(1):55-68.

you quit. Can you do without it? Or do you find yourself in a lethargic and cranky state? If so, withholding your normal consumption of coffee on the first days of quitting could induce caffeine withdrawal, compounding (as well as confounding) nicotine withdrawal![1] If you plan to have coffee on your quit day, be prepared to experiment until you find an amount that you feel comfortable with.

Alcohol

Alcohol's a powerful trigger for most smokers. Plus, have enough drinks and you'll likely let your guard down and smoke! Stay away from alcohol for the first three days. If you are able to, stay away from alcohol for a week.

Water

Many sources say you should drink lots of water - about two litres or half a gallon a day - when you quit. Doing so will 'satisfy oral cravings' and clear and repair your system. I don't know about oral cravings but drinking plenty of water is a good idea in itself. In fact, you should already be drinking two litres of water daily because you're smoking - to clear and repair your system.

Beware of dropping sugar levels

Smoking alters our body's natural blood sugar regulating mechanism. This mechanism may need a few days to regain its

1 Caffeine and nicotine withdrawal symptoms are starkly similar i.e. fatigue, irritability, difficulty concentrating, flu-like symptoms and more. Visit Johns Hopkins Bayview Campus' web site for more information - www.caffeinedependence.org.

natural rhythm when we quit. Our performance and moods may be affected during this period.

Smoking triggers the release of your body's store of sugar into your blood. Your brain senses the higher blood sugar levels and regulates hormones to curb your appetite. This system disappears when you stop smoking. Your brain and body need to re-establish its natural blood sugar regulating mechanism – the one you had before you started smoking. This takes about three days.

Meanwhile, your blood sugar levels may not be in synch with the needs of the rest of your body. You may feel weak, dizzy or have trouble concentrating because your brain is not getting enough sugar. At the same time, your appetite improves remarkably. In the past, you enjoyed having a cigarette after a meal. The cigarette raised your blood sugar levels in less than a minute thereby suppressing your appetite. You felt full.

Now that you've quit, it takes at least 20 minutes for your food to be converted into sugar and delivered to your brain. During this time, your brain is anticipating a quick rise in blood sugar like it used to when you smoked. When this fails to happen, your brain regulates your hormones to maintain your appetite (to raise your blood sugar levels). This is why you will tend to have a much better appetite when you quit.

Is there anything you can do to ease the periods of low blood sugar levels? Try milk, cheese, apples, fruit juices or glucose-based products such as Dextrosol and Glucolin. Rough it out if you feel up to it.

Colleagues and friends offer you cigarettes to test you

You'll inevitably have to inform your smoker friends and colleagues that you've stopped smoking. Some of them will offer you cigarettes *because* you've stopped (many smokers poke fun at new ex-smokers this way. I used to be one of those fools). Turn them down as affably as you're able to. Feel sorry for them. Be glad that you're no longer misguided and don't have to smoke any longer.

During the first week of your quit, avoid colleagues and friends when they smoke. If you are not able to - maybe your partner or housemates smoke - remind yourself of the reasons you are quitting (see pages 4 and 5). If you have to spend a substantial amount of time with people who smoke, take it as another challenge you're going to overcome. Also, if your partner smokes and isn't quitting, focus on yourself quitting first. You'll set a good example whether your intention's to be one or not.

Don't get into arguments with your smoker friends and colleagues - remember, calm and cool - if they try to taunt or tease you into smoking. They'll eventually tire and stop if they don't get a response. If, however, they see that they're getting to you - you stiffen up, glare, grumble, raise your voice etc. - they're likely to go on, to see what it'll take to get you to smoke again.

Think of it from this perspective - your colleagues and friends may be trying to get you to smoke because they're afraid of losing someone to smoke with or bum cigarettes from. Be patient, it'll take a little time for them to accept that you're now a non-smoker.

Know that you're going to have to spend some time managing your relationships with your smoker friends and colleagues. Several may try to tempt you every now and then. Ignoring their taunts or changing the subject usually works. Experiment to see what works for you. If your friends remain difficult for weeks or months, you might want to consider changes in your social life.

Feeling stressed?

When you were a smoker, you habitually felt like smoking whenever you felt stressed. We saw on page 11 how this came about. Smoking cigarettes to relieve stress is obviously self-defeating, so forget it as an option.

You might try some interim measures during the first few days, such as breathing exercises,[1] chewing gum or having a little comfort food such as chocolate.* Do they help? At best they provide some distraction and temporary relief. They're not, however, going to make your stress inducing problems go away.

When you experience stress, take a step back and examine what's causing it. Try to tackle the problem. Ask friends or colleagues for help. Look up the WWW or books for solutions. Recognise that some problems can be acted upon and solved. Others are outside of our control. We learn to accept these and live with them.

You may find this approach hard at first. Previously, you'd try to run from the problem, or distract yourself by

1 Refer to *Emotional Intelligence 2.0* by Travis Bradberry, Jean Greaves and Patrick Lencioni for an excellent description of how to *Breathe Right.*

* Comfort food is optional. Use your own judgement as to what feels right for you.

smoking. Now you may feel *more* stress facing your problems head on. Do your best. The more successful you are in tackling them, the more confident and in control you'll feel. When this happens, you will feel less stress and better about yourself on the whole.

Unable to concentrate

Some smokers have problems concentrating during the first few days of quitting. If you're one of them, try cheese, chocolate, milk, apples, fruit juices, glucose-based products or caffeine (be more cautious about caffeine). Take more brain foods such as fish and essential fatty acids to boost your concentration levels.

Adults are generally able to concentrate on a task for about 45 minutes after which our focus starts to wane. Take 5- to 10-minute breaks. Walk around, stretch, get yourself a drink or go chat with someone for a while.

Caveat: You may follow the advice above and still find it hard to concentrate. Yes - it can be a pain! Try to take it on the chin if this happens. It's one of those annoyances we go through when making a transition. Just as it can be a pain losing weight, starting over in a new career, renovating the house, having to go through surgery, _______________, and _______________ (fill in the blanks), it can be troublesome the first couple of days when we stop smoking. The good thing is that you don't have to do too much besides accepting the interim disruption and not smoking. Your body will sort out everything else on its own. Then, several days later it'll hit you that your brain's functioning normally again.

Treat yourself

You're going to have more money now that you're not wasting it on cigarettes. You could save it for a rainy day or you could give yourself more treats. Go out more often for dinner, watch more movies, drink more wine or buy more stuff with the extra money you have. Give yourself a treat for doing what you said you would. Or just live better because you can. Just don't tell yourself you're giving yourself these treats in lieu of having 'given up' smoking. Here's why: Let's say you decide to treat yourself to more massages and more wine for not smoking. It feels good at first, but the novelty eventually wears out. You start wondering if your new treats are really worth the cigarettes you 'gave up' after all. What happens next? You're likely to deliberate between more treats, newer treats, or your previous default choice - smoking!

So, do be kind and good to yourself. Don't associate treats (or anything else) with your past cigarette dependency.

Feel a sudden urge to smoke?

As you're happily going about life not smoking, you:

* encounter one of your triggers and feel the urge to smoke;
* see someone smoking and feel like smoking yourself;
* suddenly think of smoking out of nowhere.

You realise in each case you can't smoke anymore. You think it's not fair - everyone else who wants to is smoking - but you can't. You start feeling depressed and wish you could smoke again. Don't despair. Try the following measures - they work:

1. Remember why you want to remain an ex-smoker.

- In their youth, smokers were duped into thinking smoking would make them trendier, more urbane, cooler, etc. than non-smokers. *Many are no wiser despite advancing in age and experience. They continue hanging onto this archaic portrayal of smokers.*
- Smokers were fooled - and continue being fooled - into thinking:
  - smoking gives them pleasure (when the 'pleasure' is actually temporary relief from tobacco craving).
  - cigarettes help them concentrate when all they do is alleviate the mini-withdrawal symptoms that impede concentration.
  - cigarettes relieve stress when they actually cause more stress (not only to the smoker but to non-smokers around them as well).
- To top it all, smokers grew attached to their cigarettes, likening them to friends.
- About *seven out of 10 of the smokers you come across every day wish they could quit but are unable to.* Most have tried several times but failed on each attempt. They carry on smoking:
  - trying to rationalise their addiction;
  - procrastinating indefinitely or;
  - feeling trapped by their cigarette addiction.
- Remember how, when you were younger, you let yourself be seduced into learning to smoke. You did it regularly enough that you eventually became addicted to nicotine. Along the way, you picked up ideas, attitudes and feelings

that conspired to keep you smoking. It was about then that you got hooked! You tried (and tried and tried) but just couldn't get yourself to stop smoking. After much time and effort, you finally got yourself out of that hole.

❄ ❄ ❄ ❄ ❄

Stay clear of cigarettes from now on! Be glad that you don't have your tobacco addiction anymore.

Think of all the trouble you're going to have to go through if you fall back in again!

❄ ❄ ❄ ❄ ❄

2. Remind yourself not smoking is a small sacrifice you are happy to make.

If you're quitting for someone else, remind yourself that you've already made lots of sacrifices for this person, and not smoking is just another one of these sacrifices. *It's a small sacrifice you're happy to make.* You'll get a warm fuzzy feeling inside if you mean it. This is good - it'll take the edge off the urge to smoke.

3. Manipulate the thoughts urging you to smoke.

Manipulate your thoughts as described below when you feel like smoking. These are surprisingly effective - try them!

- **Manipulating cigarette images:**
  - Imagine flicking an unlit cigarette so that it summersaults harmlessly out of the window or flies off into the horizon.
  - Visualise ants making off with an imaginary cigarette. You see it moving along on the floor, disappearing

under the door and then it's gone.

  - If you are driving, imagine knocking down an adult-sized cigarette with your car.

- **Mentally deflecting the urge elsewhere:** When you think, "I want a cigarette", look around you and select something. Suppose you chose a flower in a vase. Imagine it is the flower saying, "I want a cigarette" (instead of you wanting one). If you're outdoors and select a fire hydrant, imagine the fire hydrant saying "Gimme a cigarette!"

Manipulating our thoughts and urges to smoke may seem silly and nonsensical. Nonetheless, do try some of the examples or make up your own when the opportunity arises. You'll be surprised at how well they work.

When you direct your urges to smoke into these unlikely scenarios, you take control and actively influence the situation rather than letting the situation control you. You'll likely feel better as a result. More importantly, when you do any of the above effectively, you draw your attention away from the negative feelings that arise. More often than not, after just one attempt, your cigarette craving dissipates and your despair dissolves into nothingness. You feel calm and in control again.

❄ ❄ ❄ ❄ ❄

PART 5

STAYING A NON-SMOKER

Life as a non-smoker again - Day 1 to Day 3

If you stayed off cigarettes for 24 hours - beautiful! You started out great and are now 10 times more likely to quit smoking! Keep up the great work! You should be really proud of yourself! Why not reward yourself with a (non-alcoholic) treat? If you've not already done so, now's the time to tell your friends and family that you've stopped smoking and have just made it through the first day without cigarettes.

Stay cool. In Days 2 and 3, continue noticing how novel and interesting not having to smoke anymore feels, especially in the presence of your past triggers.

Day 4 to Week 3

It tends to get noticeably easier on Day 4 or Day 5. Either way, hang in there! If you drink, you might want to try visiting the pub or bar after not smoking for a week. Notice how novel it feels being able to enjoy your drink while not smoking. Soak it in.

Some ex-smokers get tingling sensations in their arms and legs. Some experience flu-like symptoms including coughing, runny nose and feeling drowsy. Many do not. If these happen to you, remind yourself that this is good - your body is doing repair work and cleansing itself of all the toxins the cigarettes have being putting in all these years. After a couple of days, they will disappear forever.

By the end of the first week, you should have fewer thoughts and less intense urges to smoke. You'll feel much more confident you're going to succeed staying off cigarettes permanently. You may 'forget your cigarettes' when leaving home or the office and then pleasantly realise you don't need them any longer. The nagging worry of not having enough cigarettes has disappeared. You know you don't need them and realise that you're free of them! This is a freedom you've not experienced since you got hooked on cigarettes.

Week 3 Onwards

You've been free of cigarettes for more than 3 weeks now. You feel fine without them and hardly think of smoking. You're just cruising along. You should know, however, that you'll continue getting urges to smoke every now and then. Some of these may turn out to be *huge* (see the next page).

Many smokers dream they started smoking again. I had a few. Some of these dreams seemed so vivid and real that it took me some time to affirm that they were only dreams. Though they may be disturbing, don't read into them. They don't mean anything.

If you've never been the top five percent of anything, here's a great chance to do something about it. All you need to do is keep this up. Simply stay the course and, before you know it, you'll be among the five percent of smokers who will stop this year. Behind you will be the 95 percent who tried but failed. This will be quite an achievement - something to be very pleased about!

At various times between the end of Week 1 and the end of Month 2, you may be a little curious as to whether you're ‘cured’.* If you’re considering testing this hypothesis by trying a cigarette – DON’T because it’ll very probably re-ignite each of your smoking influences again. If that happens, it’s back to cigarette dependency! It’s just not worth the trouble.

Help! I’m having a Colossal Cigarette Attack!

Things are going well. You’ve not smoked for two, three or six months. It’s smooth sailing.

One day, out of the blue, you feel sad and empty. It’s like there’s suddenly a dark, gaping void within you. You have an overwhelming urge to smoke. You wonder if you’re really a confirmed smoker after all.

This is when you’ll be at your most vulnerable throughout the whole programme. Don’t give in, and stay calm. Transform your smoking urge into something frivolous and silly (or do something else that has worked well for you in the past). The desire to smoke will disappear as suddenly as it occurred. Though these are quite unsettling - enough to unsettle you to smoke again - they do not happen often.

Why *do* these happen? During the early stages of quitting, you were generally vigilant to overcome everyday situations that triggered the urge to smoke. Here you weren’t so ready. You likely came across an unusual trigger, one that you don’t come across often in everyday life.

If you’ve not travelled overseas since quitting, the duty free shop - where you used to love dropping into for your carton of cheap cigarettes - could be a powerful trigger.

Did you frequently smoke and have alcoholic drinks when-

* Incidentally, this is a signpost that the hardest part’s over and that it’s mostly blue skies from here on. You’re curious because it feels odd that you’ve stopped having the urge or inclination to smoke. That is, *you have stopped wanting to smoke!*

ever you checked into a hotel? If so, be prepared for another powerful attack when you're about to have a drink in your hotel room. Are you visiting your parent's home, where you used to smoke? Watch out for another attack while in your old room, the porch or balcony if that's where you frequently smoked.

The good thing is that these are conditioned responses. Every time you do not respond to these massive urges, that is, by not smoking, you desensitise yourself to them. Manage them and they stop altogether after one or two encounters.

Oops! Didn't quite make it!

What if you sneaked in one or more cigarettes anytime during your quit? Things were going smoothly but you let your guard down or something threw you off balance. You gave in and smoked.

Well, I'm sure you tried your best and it was a good try. If at any time during your Positive Quit you slip and smoke one or more cigarettes, take a step back and consider: "Do I want to carry on with my quit?" If you're confident you'll able to despite this setback, if you're sure you'll still be able to succeed, by all means do go on. If, however, you feel you're on shaky ground, it's okay to try afresh in the not-too-distant future.

Hopefully it doesn't come to this. Follow the advice here and it most likely won't. Then, before you know it, you'll be enjoying life as a non-smoker again.

The advantages of being a non-smoker again

Set an alert on your mobile phone to 'revisit page 54 of the PQ Manual' about six months from now. Tick those benefits and advantages that apply to you. You'll feel good about your progress and this will help see you through the rest of the year and beyond!

- ☐ I breathe much easier
- ☐ My sore throat and smoker's cough are gone
- ☐ My periodic chest pains have disappeared
- ☐ I worry much less about getting lung cancer or other dreadful smoking-related diseases
- ☐ I'm happy I'm not polluting my body anymore
- ☐ Food and drink taste much better
- ☐ I had my teeth cleaned and they've never looked better
- ☐ My complexion has improved
- ☐ I feel more attractive
- ☐ I feel more energetic and alive
- ☐ I have more money now and I'm happy to stop wasting it
- ☐ My partner is glad I've quit smoking
- ☐ My kids are happy that I've stopped smoking
- ☐ The baby doesn't have to deal with my first- or second-hand smoke
- ☐ I've stopped having to make excuses - to others and to myself - about needing to smoke
- ☐ I've stopped worrying about being able to smoke as a guest at someone's house
- ☐ I'm glad I don't get dirty looks for polluting the air
- ☐ I don't feel like a social outcast any longer

- ☐ I feel more in control of myself
- ☐ I feel more mature
- ☐ I noticed that some people have more respect for me for successfully quitting
- ☐ I used to feel weak being addicted to tobacco. Now I feel strong!
- ☐ I feel proud about my accomplishment - it's a massive achievement for me!
- ☐ I feel more confident and satisfied with myself for quitting
- ☐ I've made other significant, positive changes in my life since I stopped smoking
- ☐ My future feels much brighter now
- ☐ I feel so much freer!
    - ☐ I've stopped worrying if I have enough cigarettes
    - ☐ I've stopped having to carry a pack of cigarettes with me wherever I go
    - ☐ I've freed myself of my addiction!
- ☐ Wooo hooo!!!

Other benefits I've enjoyed:

____

____

____

____

____

____

POSITIVELY QUIT'S SMOKING MODEL

The Positively Quit model is simple. We all start with a blank slate. Smokers, however, unwittingly create 'agents' that start and then keep them smoking. Positively Quit's goal is to arm smokers with effective tools to undermine each agent's hold over them.

The 'Cognitive Agent'. The Cognitive Agent is a product of the thoughts and ideas smokers have about smoking. This agent is powered by ideas – the ideas we acquired concerning smoking. Some ideas were planted into our heads by the media, our friends and siblings. Others we created on our own watching others smoke. Examples include the impression that smoking is fun, looks cool and turns boys into men.

We represent the Cognitive Agent with a silver spring. It started small at first – mostly as an intellectual curiosity. Then, as we smoked our way through life, as we picked up opinions about cigarette brands, about smoking in general and about ourselves as smokers, our Cognitive Agent grew in resilience and strength. Those smoking-related notions that we accepted as true eventually influenced the way we behave. If you believe smoking relieves stress, imagine your Cognitive Agent *stretch* each time you feel stressed. This creates an additional tension - tension for you to smoke.

Lighting a cigarette or removing the source of stress relieves the tension.

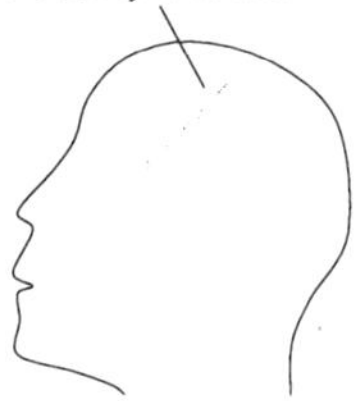

Note that your Cognitive Agent is an artificial, self-inflicted stressor. If, for some reason, you are not able to smoke when under stress, you have the original source of stress *plus* the added stress of 'needing a smoke' (but not being able to).

A stubborn and deep-seated agent. Beliefs and ideas, especially those held for a long time, tend to be stubbornly fixed. Smokers, in particular, tend to be fixed in their beliefs about smoking.

What was your response to the following (from page 6)?

- ☐ I am a light smoker
- ☐ I am a medium smoker
- ☐ I am a heavy smoker

If you chose, for example, 'I am a heavy smoker', you will tend to continue thinking and *behaving* in ways you think heavy smokers do. To stop wanting to smoke, you'll need to change how you think about smoking and about yourself as a smoker (hence, the 'thinking person's guide to stop smoking' may be the most appropriate approach to quit smoking). Can you imagine thinking you have stopped smoking but still believe, deep down, that you're a heavy smoker? These thoughts not only do not go along, they clash! Only one or the other will prevail (and it's usually the one that we think will make us feel better).

Likewise, believing that smoking relieves stress makes staying off cigarettes difficult because you'll be tempted to smoke every time you feel under pressure. Conversely, quitting is less demanding when you don't have these misinformed, smoking perpetuating thoughts and instead think:

"Smoking doesn't relieve stress - it actually creates more of it. Also, I am a non-smoker now and I have nothing to do with cigarettes."

The 'Chemical Agent' is represented by a black spring. It is our nicotine addiction. Imagine this addiction as a tiny black spring developing somewhere in your head when you started smoking. It starts insignificant and weak. You feed it with every cigarette you smoke, making it grow larger and stronger.

Chemical Agent
"Smoke a cigarette"

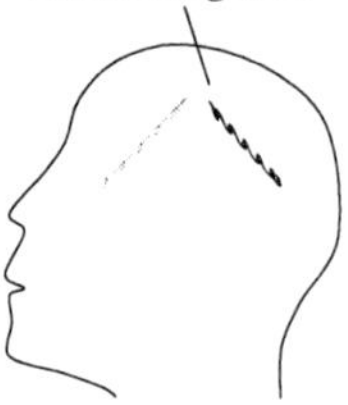

Eventually, like the Cognitive Agent, this spring starts to exert pressure upon you. Not smoking at your regular intervals makes this black spring stretch. This creates tension and discomfort. When you light a cigarette, the spring eases and lets you feel comfortable again.

This addiction was not something you were born with. You created it when you started smoking. More importantly, you weaken it simply by not smoking. Stop smoking long enough and this agent will die off and disappear altogether.

The 'Emotions Agent' is represented by a grey spring. It characterises our emotional attachment to smoking. For example, you might derive what seems like pleasure and a sense of completion from smoking after meals. Before going on a flight, you might feel delight buying cheap cigarettes by the carton at the duty free shop. On the other hand, the thought of not being able to smoke for extended

Emotions Agent
Relaxed / Tense
'Pleasure' / Distress

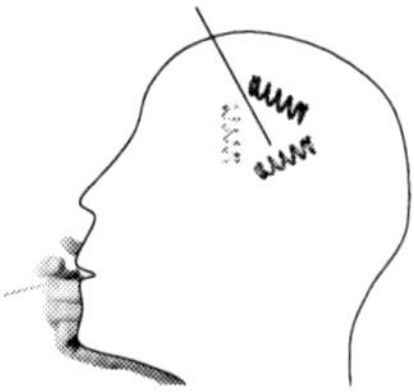

periods, say on a long haul flight, might leave you feeling somewhat distressed.

A Powerful Agent. The Emotions Agent may seem fairly innocuous, but it's probably the most 'persuasive' and powerful of the three agents. Some smokers who smoked their last cigarette and then told themselves "That's it – that's my last cigarette forever" have reported feeling:

"Like my best friend died"

"Completely depressed"

"Like a part of myself – an arm or a leg – was being cut off and lost forever"

The smoker's natural tendency would be to attempt to stop these extremely unpleasant feelings. The easiest way to do this is by *not* quitting. She would therefore have a strong urge to reach for and light a cigarette. Even if a smoker managed to resist these urges when quitting, similar emotions might arise again in the future, tempting her to smoke. For instance, she may feel envious when she sees friends lighting up outside after dinner. Or she may feel distressed at not being able to smoke under a tight deadline, especially when she sees her colleagues doing so. *Quitting clearly becomes easier when one is able to effectively manage these and other similar emotions.*

Positively Quit does this in two ways. One route is via a pre-emptive blanket approach. Positive Quitters are strongly advised to go into their quit feeling excited about the whole affair. At the same time, they're to stay calm and cool during the first few days. When we maintain these emotional states, we crowd out fear, depression, irritation and other negative affective states that may accompany smoking cessation. Quitting becomes more pleasant and easier.

The second approach to manage negative emotions is by *taking control of our thoughts.* Our ex-smoker friend described above would feel much better if she reminded herself why her friends are smoking after dinner – because of their mistaken beliefs and because their addicted bodies crave nicotine. Even if she had tried explaining to her friends the nature of their addiction, they probably wouldn't listen (until they're good and ready, smokers are generally content to remain misguided and addicted). Our friend would naturally feel sorry for them instead of feeling jealous and bitter. She'd likely feel glad she's stopped smoking.

THE MODEL EXPLAINS OLDER QUIT METHODS

Cold Turkey. The smoker attempts to simply stop smoking for good. This approach can be difficult because the person's thoughts, feelings and nicotine addiction all act to get him to light a cigarette! If he stays off cigarettes, his nicotine addiction progressively goes away. However, the residual Cognitive and Emotions Agents *may still push the ex-smoker to smoke.* This leaves him at risk. If these misguided thoughts and feelings about smoking are not resolved, they may tempt the ex-smoker, who quit smoking months or years ago, to suddenly start again.

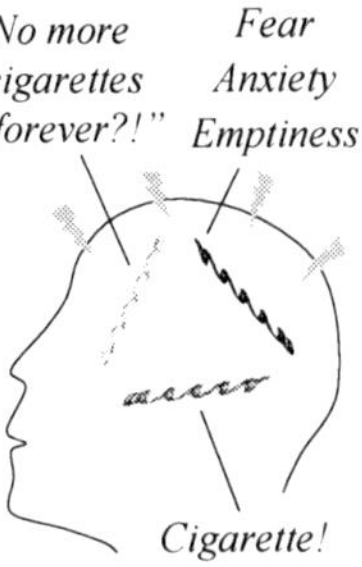

Cutting Down. Cutting down (tapering) involves gradually reducing the number of cigarettes you smoke each day, until you eventually do not need any. The problem here is that the smoker is *still consuming nicotine which continues to reinforce his physical craving.* The Cognitive and Emotions Agents also remain. Delaying nicotine gratification increases the appetite for cigarettes. This makes smoking even more rewarding. Instead of becoming less desirable, cutting down increases the craving for cigarettes.

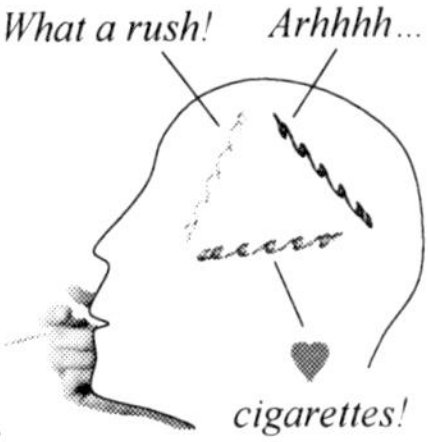

Nicotine Replacement Therapy (NRT). The smoker uses a nicotine patch, inhaler, nasal spray or gum to help wean her off cigarettes. The Positively Quit model predicts the following problems with NRT:

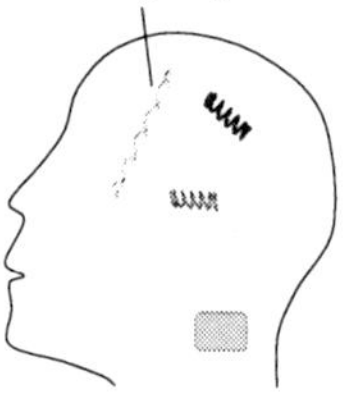

- The Cognitive and Emotions Agents are *not treated or managed.* These may trigger urges to smoke in the near or distant future.
- The smoker is still consuming nicotine. Thus, she continues to feed her addiction. What she is doing is *shifting her nicotine dependency* from the cigarette to the NRT device.
- Quitting with NRT products may reinforce the Cognitive Agent: If a smoker comes to rely upon NRT to minimise urges to smoke, she may conclude she'll need NRT each time she has the urge to smoke. As long as she thinks this, she'll be unsure she will be able to stay off NRT or cigarettes. This leaves her susceptible to smoking again:

  "I needed patches to quit.. I feel like smoking now but don't have a patch with me! What do I do?"

Positively Quit. The Positively Quit position is that most smokers have misguided beliefs and feelings about smoking. It is these wrong beliefs and emotions - rather than a nicotine addiction - that make staying off cigarettes especially difficult.

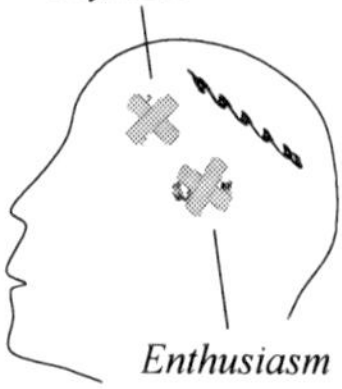

In a nutshell, Positively Quit works to:

- help smokers dispel myths and change their attitudes towards smoking;
- help smokers manage their emotions;
- arm the quitter with tools to prevent relapses.

The only issue left is the nicotine addiction. The Positive Quitter resolves this simply by not smoking. Only when he's stopped for good *and* has corrected his misguided thoughts and feelings about smoking, will his smoking problems be fully resolved.

Acknowledgements

I'd like to thank Desmond Soon, Loretta Lopez, Tess Votto Haranda, Kathleen Karabanov, Mary Ann Fields, Laura Throop and John Chancellor for their help and suggestions. Thanks to Debra, my wife, for listening, letting her brain be stormed and for being patient with me. Special mention goes to our kids, Ethan and Ella, who provided the impetus for me to stop smoking (and thus, without whom, there'd be no Positively Quit!). Finally, a big thank you to everyone who has taken the time to give feedback and lent her or his support to the Positively Quit Manual.

A quick word from the manual writer

I smoked my first cigarette in 1984, in a karaoke bar in Kashima, Japan. With plenty of support from friends, I went on to smoke a packet of cigarettes a day for the next 20 years.

When our first child, Ethan, arrived in 1999, I started the first of several attempts to quit for good. I tried going 'cold turkey', 'cutting down' and other methods but failed. I wasn't even able to go a full day without cigarettes each time. After much research about smoking and addiction, I finally quit in April 2004. This time around, quitting was relatively easy and undemanding, after all my misguided views about smoking were put right and then using the steps described here to stay off cigarettes. I hope that following the advice here helps you quit smoking without a hitch as well.

All the best!

Appendix - Recommended personal growth books

You're all psyched up. You're sure you'll quit or already have. There's an extra bounce in your step. You're ready to do more. You're ready to *be* more. Read these books to become happier and more productive.

The Success Principles(TM): How to Get from Where You Are to Where You Want to Be by Jack Canfield and Janet Switzer

The Happiness Hypothesis: Finding Modern Truth in Ancient Wisdom by Jonathan Haidt

Happiness: A Guide to Developing Life's Most Important Skill by Matthieu Ricard and Daniel Goleman

Healthy at 100: The Scientifically Proven Secrets of the World's Healthiest and Longest-Lived Peoples by John Robbins

Six Myths About the Good Life: Thinking About What Has Value by Joel J. Kupperman

Emotional Intelligence 2.0 by Travis Bradberry, Jean Greaves, and Patrick M. Lencion

Bonds That Make Us Free: Healing Our Relationships, Coming to Ourselves by C. Terry Warner

The Seven Principles for Making Marriage Work: A Practical Guide from the Country's Foremost Relationship Expert by John M. Gottman and Nan Silver

Hold Me Tight: Seven Conversations for a Lifetime of Love by Sue Johnson

Are You Ready to Succeed? Unconventional Strategies to Achieving Personal Mastery in Business and Life by Srikumar S. Rao

The Anatomy of Peace: Resolving the Heart of Conflict by Arbinger Institute

One Small Step Can Change Your Life: The Kaizen Way by Robert Maurer

What I Wish I Knew When I Was 20: A Crash Course on Making Your Place in the World by Tina Seelig

Crucial Conversations: Tools for Talking When Stakes are High by Kerry Patterson, Joseph Grenny, Ron McMillan, and Al Switzler

The Happiness Trap: How to Stop Struggling and Start Living by Russ Harris and Steven Hayes

9 Things You Simply Must Do to Succeed in Love and Life: A Psychologist Learns from His Patients What Really Works and What Doesn't by Dr. Henry Cloud

The Sedona Method: Your Key to Lasting Happiness, Success, Peace and Emotional Well-Being by Hale Dwoskin and Jack Canfield

The Magic of Thinking Big by David Schwartz

Life's Greatest Lessons: 20 Things That Matter by Hal Urban

The Anger Trap: Free Yourself from the Frustrations that Sabotage Your Life by Les Carter and Frank Minirth

100 Ways To Motivate Yourself: Change Your Life Forever by Steve Chandler

Lightning Source UK Ltd.
Milton Keynes UK
UKOW031836060912

198608UK00010B/1/P

9 789810 874179